I0413427

The Oscarian Theory Series

Keith Oscar Williams

The Oscarian Theory Series

Table of Contents

Acknowledgment

First and foremost, I give honor to my Lord and Savior, Jesus Christ, for granting me the insight and inspiration to write this book. Without Him, none of my gifts would be worth pursuing.

I dedicate this book to my loving wife, Sheona B. Williams, whose unwavering support has fueled my passion for writing poetry over the years. Her love burns deeply for me, even in moments when I fail to notice it, and for that, I am eternally grateful.

I extend my deepest appreciation to my spiritual mentors and friends who have believed in me and my ministry. Special thanks to all those mentioned in my stories—your encouragement, through both my good and difficult experiences, has given me the strength to press forward. I am honored to have been part of your lives.

I also wish to express gratitude to my psychology professors—Dr. Clay Evans, Dr. David Sullivan, and Dr. George Moretz—who inspired me to research and develop my personal counseling and psychotherapy theory. After years of struggling with mental illness, I have become deeply committed to spreading awareness of the condition and exploring natural treatment options. May God continue to enrich your careers until our Savior returns.

To my parents, Albert Williams Sr. and Dorothy Leon Williams—I know that, for years, you could not understand why I was so driven to write. After my first book was published, you finally saw the depth of my passion. Thank you for believing in me and supporting my journey. I love you both dearly.

To the church family at the Church of God in True Holiness in Fredericksburg, VA—thank you for embracing me and my ministry. Your unwavering faith and support have given me strength, and I will always cherish the memories—both joyful and challenging—that we have shared. It is my prayer that God continues to uplift the church and all who attend. You will never be forgotten.

Finally, to Myra Fox—I must single you out, as God has blessed you with an extraordinary gift as a writer, a talent I am privileged to share with you. Your dedication has inspired me to keep writing and striving for excellence. I know that everything will align for you because God has placed great faith in your journey.

The Oscarian Group Planning Approach (2005)

My role in the group is to help the members be able to change the way they are speaking and behaving towards oneself and others, be able to interact back into society, and unlock the member's must hidden thoughts and actions.

I would the group to realize their problems and how to effectively solve them.

It would help me if the me and members of the group to form the contract. That way, we can work together and interact with one another. I believe from that point; the group and I can create a strong bond. The contract will consist of simple rules to make sure that the group and the sessions run smoothly.

My letter of informed consent would include the following: the purpose and objectives of the group, what are the expectations from the counselor and the counselees, what can and cannot be said outside the group, rules that will promote tolerance and awareness, and all rights and responsibilities for each member of the group.

The best way to determine whether I have to skills to lead a group is to observe another group leader through mentoring and practice until I have mastered the concepts and theories taught.

The focus of my group is to mend broken families and households back together and making sure that they stay together.

I would accept volunteered and non-volunteered members because I realize that both of them need help. I have a passion to helping people solve their problems.

It doesn't matter what size the family is: a family with one parent, a family with two parents, and an unlimited number of children. The family must be willing to go to counseling to work out their issues, and everyone family must participate in the sessions. I take a personal interest in working with broken families because I'm able to handle the dilemma of my own family who see me as a beacon of light. It can get stressful sometimes, but I believe I'm able to perform the task well. There can be a split between the husbands and wives and then the children. Then we can bring the family back together from some exercises on a larger scale.

The first procedure in dealing with broken families are to use the division of family method. In this method, I would divide the family into three parts: the father, the mother, and the children. The purpose of this process is the address the needs and concerns from each part of the family. The second procedure in dealing with broken families is to use the unity of family method. In this method, I would make a report to the family about the individual needs and concerns and ask the family members to respond in a healthy way. The last procedure in dealing with broken families is to use the opposite family behavior method. In this method, I would attempt to create several exercise and examples on have to be a family that can do the opposite of what they were doing before. For example, if the mother and father were arguing violently, I would show them how to have healthy arguments. Furthermore, if the children are disrupted at home, I can provide insight on things to keep them occupied so they won't get into trouble.

Based on the severity of the situation(s), I would create a plan of action cover as much time as the family needs to get back on track. I would write down everything so I can keep an eye on their progress. These reports will determine whether the family had met the objectives or the group needs more time to work out new or existing issues.

To determine whether or not the members master the skills necessary to promote healthy problem solving, there would be homework assignments and quizzes.

The Oscarian Theory for the Existence of God (2006)

Introduction

In H.J. McCloskey's article, On Being an Atheist, he is trying to prove that the existence of God is not true; having many claims why atheism is an easier concept to understand than theism. After being a part of the arena of philosophy, we can finally develop a simple why to explain the existence of God in a way that everyone can understand. The theist believed that atheism is a cold, uncommon belief that places ourselves as our own supreme being, looking to ourselves as the master of our domain and we can do as we please without interference from any outside forces. The research conducted over the past few months will simplify the aspects of God's existence and why McCloskey's claim to atheism will lead many people astray from the truth.

Key Concepts

<u>The nouthetic-biblical view of God's existence</u>

Man was created by God in His image (Genesis 1.26, 27) as a three-fold being (I Thessalonians 5.23): body (I Corinthians 12.12), soul (Genesis 2.7), and spirit (Romans 8.16), which play important roles in the way we think, feel, and act. It was appropriate for God to design man this way so he can be more represented as an image of Himself.

The concept of man having a three-fold being came from Sigmund Freud's theory of psychoanalysis (1895/1966b). Both presuppositions are so similar in function and behavior that it's one of the main assumptions adopted by the Nouthetic-Biblical Counseling theory. The body is identical to the id, the spirit is identical to the superego, and the soul is identical to the ego. Frank Minirth (2003) had the same concept about the relationship of the body, soul, and spirit with Freud's concept of the id, the ego, and the superego (Freud, 1923/1962).

The body was formed from the dust of the Earth (Genesis 2.7), which became corrupted by sin (Genesis 3.19), which resulted in bad behavior and mental distress. However, we have been redeemed by Jesus Christ (Romans 5.8) as a source to help us deal with our problems. The body must be renewed daily from sin and corruption (II Corinthians 4.16). We must strive for perfection or good behavior through the power of the Holy Spirit and support from people God place in our life (e.g. the counselor, the therapist, the pastor, etc.). The body or the corruptible part of man resembles Sigmund Freud's immoral part of man's personality, the id. The id seeks pleasure and avoids pain at all cost through the inner motivational source of man, the libido. According to Freud (1923), the libido is the sexual drive of man; however, it could be referred to as the flesh, the part of man that seeks to satisfy its needs without any regards for anyone or anything.

The spirit is the incorruptible part of man that must bear witness to the Spirit of God (Romans 8.16). By connecting the human spirit with God's spirit, we are made one with Him (Ephesians 4.1-6). A perfect match for this drive of man is what Freud (1923) called the moral agent or the superego. The spirit tries to place the body or flesh under subjection just as the superego tries to govern the id in Freud's psychoanalysis theory (1925). There will always be a constant struggle between the body and spirit just like the id will always fight against the superego for control of man.

The soul is the thinking, feeling, and consciousness of self (1 Corinthians 2.14, 15) as having a free well (Joshua 24.15), and is capable of making decisions. God has given humans a mind to think, reason, and obtain knowledge and wisdom. Freud's concept of the ego has similar traits as the soul. Just like the ego, the soul is the thinker and planner of what the rest of man must do (1923b). The soul also checks the motives of the spirit and flesh just as the ego checks the impulses of the id and the superego. The final choice is made by the soul, which determines how we think, feel, and act (behave). Negative behavior results in stress, guilt, punishment, and mental anguish.

Positive behavior results in rewards, happiness, and peace.

Man is sinful in nature (Isaiah 9.6), needing a Savior to rescue him from eternal death (Romans 8.3, 4).

The nouthetic-biblical view of a worldview

A worldview is ideas, beliefs, and concepts an individual used to develop a philosophy of life. Earlier stated, the way we think and act is based on internal and external forces. Another way we think and behavior comes from our very own philosophy. A worldview deals with the following questions (Belk in, Corey, Patterson, and n.d.). McCloskey suggested that the world, the people in the world, and the events occurring in the world determines a worldview. Since McCloskey doesn't believe in the existence of God, he used the cosmological and teleological arguments to disprove that God is nonexistent. Our worldview consists of the following questions:

The question of ORIGIN
"How did life begin in the first place?"
"Where did I come from?"
The question of IDENTITY
"What does it mean to be a human?"
"Am I more important than animals?"
The question of MEANING (purpose)
"Why are we here?"
"Why am I here?"
The question of MORALITY (ethics)
"What is meant by right and wrong?"
"How should I live?"
The question of DESTINY

The Oscarian Theory Series

"Is there life after death?"
"What will happen to me when I die?"
"Will I have to answer for the choices I made and how I lived my life?"

Basic Assumptions of the Theory

In dealing with McCloskey's claim to down theism, there are several assumptions that he talked about in his paper: the existence of God, faith, and the problem of evil.

The existence of God

McCloskey claims that theism is vague, treating the concept of God as a cosmological argument, which attempts to present the case that

God's presence causes the evidence of the cosmos or the universe. In a cosmological argument, the first cause must be explained by an uncaused caused.

In other words, there must be someone or something that cause the action. How the universe did come about? Who cause the universe to exist? These are questions that McCloskey claimed that happened cosmologically by something other than God. It could be noted that McCloskey believed that there was some other force at work in creating the universe (The Big Bang Theory) and the fact that we evolved from some other creature in the animal kingdom (Evolution). What he doesn't believe is that God is the creator and ruler of the universe, but totally rejected the claim that God deity, but an intentional master of evil determines to interfere with the order of man.

The theory assumes that

There are three distinct personalities of God (the Father, the Son, and the Holy Spirit), but He is one person. Each person has three difference jobs, but they work together to accomplish one thing: to bring harmony between Him and the universe He created.

God is immaterial, meaning He is without shape or form but can be everywhere at once. McCloskey cannot grasp this concept we have human beings must see some form of substance before we believe. If you cannot see God, He doesn't exist (according to McCloskey).

God has many names and attributes that reveal to us who He is and what He does, an argument to McCloskey said to be ontological, meaning we are attempting to prove that God really does exist. McCloskey admitted that if there is a God, He must be given attributes that explain how the world was created. He rejected this concept because how can a God exist and there is evil in the world. McCloskey concluded that insecurity and arrest of the world is caused by this intentionally-muddling evil spirit. There is one problem with that statement: God is not the author of evil. McCloskey failed to realize that there is also another force that is the mastermind behind evil: Satan (the devil). Examples of names are Yahweh (cause to exist), Elohim (God Almighty), and Christos (the Messiah, the anointed one). Examples of attributes are omnipresent (everywhere at once), omniscient (knows everything known or unknown to man), and omnipotent (the most powerful being ever know that cause things to happen).

There is no other force we know of that created the universe other than God. We know this because man can never explain things our world that are unexplainable. We know that there must have been someone that caused the universe to come into existence. Scientists for years have attempted to conclude the existence only to no avail. They came up with different theories, but none of them are absolute. Only a law can be absolute. A theory can be change or amended. That is why God's law such as gravity, thermodynamics, and creation are set higher than any theory.

Faith

McCloskey defines faith as being a state of concern where the truth will be revealed in given time and claims that faith involves taking a risk, being reckless, and being irrational. McCloskey stated that having faith is evil and irrational because he claimed God is imperfect and there is no evidence of Him being perfect. In other words, he is saying that God and man can let us down. God is said to be the cause of evil when man is trying to do the right thing and man lives in the world to gain of himself only looking out for himself. McCloskey concluded that faith is not evidence of the existence of God.

The theory assumes that

Faith is the substances of things we believe are yet to come, but we hope that it will come in the near future. In other words, we believe that God will save from evil those who turn from the world and do the things His law requires, a concept McCloskey said it's impossible to do because how can we believe in something to come when we cannot see it. Faith means that we are not worried about what evil will come upon us, but to focus on the good that overshadow evil. People will see the good and know it didn't happen by one's works, but someone that cause to be: God Himself.

Faith within itself cannot prove the existence of God because there are many other factors you will need to make such a conclusion. If you talk to various Christians about the existence of God, each one will tell a different story. Some Christians will either mention who He is, what He can do, or how He changes their lives. If we stop listening to the cares this world, perhaps we can tap into the source of knowledge: God through His Holy Spirit.

Faith is proof that something will happen and we do things that cause others to believe that we can be trusted. In the natural world, when a person promises us something, we must gain their trust by doing things that signify trust. God works the same way. Sometimes, God will give us things that we don't reserve simply because of His goodness and grace. When something is promise that requires no action but trust in a person's security, it's known as unconditional faith. At other times, God promise us something with conditions so see if we really trust Him. An action that is display trust that is promised will be delivered is called conditional faith. There are risks involved being a Christian, but it will pay off in the end.

Our works doesn't save us, but our faith does. There are no actions we can do keep us from experiencing evil in our lives. Evil is present only because man seeks independence from some ruling superior, whether it's God or another god. Although we must work in order to gain the trust of God, our works will not justify us, but our faith will. We cannot be pleasing to God without faith because that tells God that we don't trust Him and we can make it on our own. If we know from past experiences how God has been faithful to us that is succulent evidence that God does exist. Even though we cannot see Him, we know He exist through other people, the world around us, and His creation of the world and our very own ideas.

The problem of evil

According to McCloskey, he believed that God is a being that created evil by interfering with man and upset the boundaries of nature. McCloskey rejected the existence of God because he questioned the perfection of His character. In other words, he saying how can God be so perfect yet He allows evil to infiltrate our world? There is nowhere in any writings that suggest that God is evil, but in most writings, God is view as a person who serves justice, but is merciful and loving. If God isn't the author of evil, then who is?

The theory assumes that

Evil came from another immaterial substance other than God Himself. McCloskey didn't look into the possibility that there could be someone else at work to promote evil and cause suffering.

Evil comes when we doing wrong or right. No matter how we act, evil will always be amongst us until the day of Jesus Christ's return. But since McCloskey doesn't believe in God, what will happen to man and nature? His argument doesn't provide an apology for this question. If we act different from the world, the world will hate us. The world expects us to act like them, the world will love us; however, if we follow God and disassociate ourselves with the world, we will experience evil.

Evil is the result of the choices we make. God has given us free will (reasoning) to decide what we do. McCloskey suggested that since we are free to do whatever we please, that God caused evil to come to the world. That is not true. God had set standards for us to live by that are superior to any natural law; however, we choose not to obey them. As a result, evil follows us.

Evil is the result of opposing views between two people. When one person disagrees with another, we have been thought to defend occur cause with all necessary even to inflict harm to someone else. McCloskey believed that God doesn't exist because evil exist for how can God exist and stop the evil around us. Evil abounds because we failed to realize that there is another force present that plead allegiance to in order to carry out evil. Anytime we oppose an idea or concept, we will be criticizing, persecuted, or even harmed. What we don't understand, we are against and what we are against, we will defend our cause even to the point of inflicting evil.

Theologians such as James Dobson, Frank Minirth, Larry Crabb, and Narramore all agree that our sinful nature is the cause of all problems we face in life. Who cause some problems in our life? We do. Why? Our actions determine the outcomes of our life, whether it's positive or negative. In fact, Dobson (1995) points out that all men are affected by sin and subject to death (Romans 5.12) and all sin and fell short of God's glory (Romans 3.23). In other words, all men, from birth, have to deal with stress, mental distress, and physical and emotional anguish because those problems were added to our nature after Adam and Eve fell in the Garden of Eden. Sin is the main reason why human beings experience hardship, pain, and distress in the world (Genesis 3.16-19). Negative behavior (i.e. depression, anxiety disorders, personality disorders, stress, and other disabilities) are inner struggles within ourselves that points directly to our sinful nature caused by forces inside or outside the self. The soul or mind is under attack constantly due to our inner struggles or outside forces that influence how we think, feel, act, and react to certain stimuli or stressors. Sigmund Freud (1924) made a great contribution to the Nouthetic-Biblical Counseling theory in the area of the inner parts of man fighting for control (p. 44). With the soul (i.e. the ego) as governor of flesh (i.e. the id) and spirit (i.e. the superego), these two parts of man are competing for attention. Whatever choice the soul makes depends on the influence of external forces (e.g. other people, Satan, God, demonic spirits, society) or internal forces (e.g. the body, the human spirit, the Holy Spirit) After a choice is made, an action or a behavior is carried out. Whether negative or positive, all behavior carries consequences; there is hope for people who seek a solution to their inner struggles or what we called in psychology mental problems. The birth, ministry, death, and resurrection of Jesus Christ provided us with a way of escape and the only hope we have to rid ourselves of our mental and emotional stress.

Conclusion

Does God truly exist? Theists know that He does, but there many claims to know that He exists. We may not be able to know everything there is to know about the existence of God, but what we know is driven by faith. We will never know everything about God nor will we be able to understand everything about Him. God is too complex, multi-dimensional, and self-existing. No writings or science can ever provide God exist. All we know if that the universe, this world, and man didn't happen by chance. There was a force most powerful than us. His name is GOD.

References

Cloninger, S. (2004). Theories of personality: Understanding persons, (4th Ed.). Pearson Education.

Corey, G. (2005). Theory and practice of counseling and psychotherapy, (7th Ed.), brooks/Cole. Thompson Learning, Inc.

Minrith, F. (2003). The minirth guide for Christian counselors. Broadman and Holman Publishers.

Towns, E. L. (2001). Theology for today. Harcourt College Publishers

Nouthetic-Biblical Counseling (January 24, 2006)

Abstract

The field of counseling and psychotherapy is facing a crisis, with many theorists seeking a way to make the therapeutic process more systematic and accessible. Through empirical research and quasi-experimental studies, Nouthetic-Biblical Counseling emerged as a structured approach to address the core reasons behind human behavior. This framework provides a comprehensive strategy for assisting clients with various mental health conditions, including depression, anxiety, schizophrenia, phobias, and other disorders.

This theory integrates psychology, theology, and philosophy, forming a unified approach that therapists and counselors can utilize to enhance their practice. While many existing counseling models offer a wide range of techniques, they often focus solely on symptom management rather than addressing the underlying causes of psychological distress. Nouthetic-Biblical Counseling seeks to bridge this gap, offering a transformative method for holistic healing and personal growth.

This revision ensures a smoother flow, eliminates redundancy, and strengthens readability while making the concepts more impact. Let me know if you'd like any adjustments!

Introduction

For decades, theorists have sought to develop a simple, systematic approach to counseling—one that classifies abnormal behaviors for effective treatment and provides consistent techniques. While foundational figures such as Sigmund Freud, Albert Ellis, and B.F. Skinner contributed groundbreaking concepts, they never aimed to integrate multiple schools of thought into a unified theory capable of addressing all forms of neurotic and psychotic disorders.

In more recent years, counselors like Lahore, Minirth, Dobson, Malony, Collins, Crabb, DeVries, Farnsworth, Kirwan, Carter, and Narramore have worked to create techniques that not only treat symptoms but also attempt to eliminate the root causes of psychological distress altogether. These Christian counselors and theorists have made outstanding contributions to psychology by bridging secular and faith-based perspectives. However, despite their efforts, no existing framework has directly tackled both symptom relief and problem eradication—until now.

Nouthetic-Biblical Counseling introduces a groundbreaking approach, uniting psychology, theology, and philosophy into a singular, cohesive theory. Developed by Keith O. Williams in 2006, this system integrates both secular and Christian counseling methodologies while incorporating personal experiences of depression and anxiety. It draws inspiration from Lawrence J. Crabb's nouthetic counseling and Jay E. Adams's biblical counseling to create a comprehensive, transformative model.

For example, Freud's concept of personality structure provides insight into the origins of neurotic and psychotic behavior. Similarly, Albert Ellis's thinking-feeling-acting framework (Ellis & Belau, 1998, 1999) serves as a foundation for understanding clients' cognitive and emotional processes. By combining these sub-concepts, Nouthetic-Biblical Counseling seeks to uncover the behaviors that stem from a person's innermost thoughts and feelings, offering a deeper, more holistic approach to healing.

The field of psychology faces a growing crisis—therapists, counselors, and theorists struggle to agree on how to effectively stop patients from repeatedly returning to treatment. While symptom management is important, it is insufficient on its own. Addressing only the physical manifestations of a psychological condition does not resolve its underlying cause. There is an urgent need for a theory that synthesizes multiple disciplines to truly uncover and eliminate the core issues clients face. Nouthetic-Biblical Counseling provides that missing link, integrating psychology, theology, and philosophy to offer a revolutionary path toward genuine, lasting healing.

Key Concepts

<u>What is counseling and what are the most essential characteristics of a helping relationship?</u>

In order for us to understand the characteristics of a helping relationship, we must be able to understand the presuppositions of the Nouthetic-Biblical Counseling theory. First, we must provide the condition for which man thinks, feels, and acts. Our comprehension of man will determine why we act the way we do. This is the first step in developing a system is needed to develop a healthy relationship between counselor and the person or group being counseled. Second, we must highlight the reasoning behind man's behavior. And last, we must use a variety of tools to help clients find themselves without actually given them significant assistance.

In general, counseling, according to psychology, is to offer guidance, direction, and consultation (using scientific techniques and spiritual guidance) in order help an individual self-actualization and the understanding of oneself in order to promote change and progress. When we seek advice from something with more experience than we do, that is a form of counseling or consultation.

With every theory of counseling and psychotherapy are key concepts, basic assumptions, the major focus of the theory, and the essential characteristics of a helping relationship.

<u>View of human nature</u>

Man was created by God in His image (Genesis 1.26, 27) as a three-fold being (I Thessalonians 5.23): body (I Corinthians 12.12), soul (Genesis 2.7), and spirit (Romans 8.16), which play important roles in the way we think, feel, and act. It was appropriate for God to design man this way so he can be more represented as an image of Himself.

The concept of man having a three-fold being came from Sigmund Freud's theory of psychoanalysis (1895/1966b). Both presuppositions are so similar in function and behavior that it's one of the main assumptions adopted by the Nouthetic-Biblical Counseling theory. The body is identical to the id, the spirit is identical to the superego, and the soul is identical to the ego. Frank Minirth (2003) had the same concept about the relationship of the body, soul, and spirit with Freud's concept of the id, the ego, and the superego (Freud, 1923/1962).

The body was formed from the dust of the Earth (Genesis 2.7), which became corrupted by sin (Genesis 3.19), which resulted in bad behavior and mental distress. However, we have been redeemed by Jesus Christ (Romans 5.8) as a source to help us deal with our problems. The body must be renewed daily from sin and corruption (II Corinthians 4.16). We must strive for perfection or good behavior through the power of the Holy Spirit and support from people God place in our life (e.g. the counselor, the therapist, the pastor, etc.).

The body or the corruptible part of man resembles Sigmund Freud's immoral part of man's personality, the id. The id seeks pleasure and avoids pain at all cost through the inner motivational source of man, the libido. According to Freud (1923), the libido is the sexual drive of man; however, it could be referred to as the flesh, the part of man that seeks to satisfy its needs without any regards for anyone or anything.

The spirit is the incorruptible part of man that must bear witness to the Spirit of God (Romans 8.16). By connecting the human spirit with God's spirit, we are made one with Him (Ephesians 4.1-6). A perfect match for this drive of man is what Freud (1923) called the moral agent or the superego. The spirit tries to place the body or flesh under subjection just as the superego tries to govern the id in Freud's psychoanalysis theory (1925). There will always be a constant struggle between the body and spirit just like the id will always fight against the superego for control of man.

The soul is the thinking, feeling, and consciousness of self (I Corinthians 2.14, 15) as having a free well (Joshua 24.15), and is capable of making decisions. God has given humans a mind to think, reason, and obtain knowledge and wisdom. Freud's concept of the ego has similar traits as the soul. Just like the ego, the soul is the thinker and planner of what the rest of man must do (1923b). The soul also checks the motives of the spirit and flesh just as the ego checks the impulses of the id and the superego. The final choice is made by the soul, which determines how we think, feel, and act (behave). Negative behavior results in stress, guilt, punishment, and mental anguish.

Positive behavior results in rewards, happiness, and peace.

Man is sinful in nature (Isaiah 9.6), needing a Savior to rescue him from eternal death (Romans 8.3, 4).

Christian counselors such as James Dobson, Frank Minirth, Larry Crabb, and Narramore all agree that our sinful nature is the cause of all problems we face in life. In fact, Dobson (1995) points out that all men are affected by sin and subject to death (Romans 5.12) and all sin and fell short of God's glory

(Romans 3.23). In other words, all men, from birth, have to deal with stress, mental distress, and physical and emotional anguish because those problems were added to our nature after Adam and Eve fell in the Garden of Eden. Sin is the main reason why human beings experience hardship, pain, and distress in the world (Genesis 3.16-19). Negative behavior (i.e. depression, anxiety disorders, personality disorders, stress, and other disabilities) are inner struggles within ourselves that points directly to our sinful nature caused by forces inside or outside the self.

The soul or mind is under attack constantly due to our inner struggles or outside forces that influence how we think, feel, act, and react to certain stimuli or stressors. Sigmund Freud (1924) made a great contribution to the Nouthetic-Biblical Counseling theory in the area of the inner parts of man fighting for control (p. 44). With the soul (i.e. the ego) as governor of flesh (i.e. the id) and spirit (i.e. the superego), these two parts of man are competing for attention. Whatever choice the soul makes depends on the influence of external forces (e.g. other people, Satan, God, demonic spirits, society) or internal forces (e.g. the body, the human spirit, the Holy Spirit) After a choice is made, an action or a behavior is carried out. Whether negative or positive, all behavior carries consequences; there is hope for people who seek a solution to their inner struggles or what we called in psychological mental problems. The birth, ministry, death, and resurrection of Jesus Christ provided us with a way of escape and the only hope we have to rid ourselves of our mental and emotional stress.

Those who seek a relationship with Christ are on the road to a magnificent healing process (Minirth, 2003).

Worldview

Every person has a worldview, whether it's secular or Christian in nature. How we think and behave is based on our own philosophy of
life.

A worldview is ideas, beliefs, and concepts an individual used to develop a philosophy of life. Earlier stated, the way we think and act is based on internal and external forces. Another way we think and behavior comes from our very own philosophy. A worldview deals with the following questions (Belk in, Corey, Patterson, and n.d.)

The question of ORIGIN
"How did life begin in the first place?"
"Where did I come from?"

The question of IDENTITY
"What does it mean to be a human?"
"Am I more important than animals?"

The question of MEANING (purpose)
"Why are we here?"
"Why am I here?"

The Oscarian Theory Series

The question of MORALITY (ethics)
"What is meant by right and wrong?"
"How should I live?"

The question of DESTINY
"Is there life after death?"
"What will happen to me when I die?"
"Will I have to answer for the choices I made and how I lived my life?"

According to the counseling process, the worldview system (Belk in, n.d.) is divided into four parts called the Oscarian Worldview System:

Interdependent delivery and interdependent action (both counselor and counselee will share in the presentation of a circumstance and make sure that all actions are carried out to solve the problem).

Interdependent delivery and independent action (the counselee and counselor will present the circumstance, but the counselee has responsible of success).

Independent delivery and interdependent action (the counselee present the circumstance, but both counselor and counselee will make sure that all actions are carried out to solve the problem).

Independent delivery and independent action (the counselor will present the circumstance and make sure that the counselee carries out the actions to solve the problem).

Basic Assumptions of the Theory

In Nouthetic-Biblical Counseling, we must provide an origin for negative behavior in order to develop a system is needed to develop a healthy relationship between counselor and the person or group being counseled.

Our behavior stems from the choices we make in our minds (i.e. the soul) and from internal (e.g. the body, the spirit) and external forces (e.g. other people, Satan, God, demonic spirits, society). Every behavior that is performed by an individual or group has positive or negative consequences. The purpose of the Nouthetic-Biblical Counseling theory is to provide positive influences for acting in a positive manner.

The term behavior refers to an action that occurs after process has been thought of or influence by. All behavior begins as a thought that is carried out by action. In other words, behavior is physical display of a thought or a series of thoughts. For example, if an individual plan to rob a bank, he will need a plan of action (thought of) and it's carried out by the parties involved (action or behavior). All behavior begins in the mind where our inner self is entertained by outside forces that influence human thinking (C.F. Lewis, n.d.).

We try to reason with our influences which aid us in making decisions (S. Freud, 1923). If we possess negative or positive thoughts, it is up to us to determine if an exit strategy is need or we continue to think about the action we want to perform or the though we want to utter from our mouths. We often plan our behavior by placing together all thoughts given to us by either ourselves or some outside influence.

Our plan of action is manifested into behavior, whether it's negative or positive. These types of behavior each has advantages and disadvantages. We must decide which one is better. There are consequences for the actions we take and must be dealt with accordingly.
If a punishment occurs, more pain and depression will occur. If a reward occurs, a sense of peace and understanding is developed in us.

Sin is the origin of all problems: physical, mental, emotional, and societal. Sin had entered into the world through a major rebellion in heaven (Revelation 12.7-10), causing God to excommunicate Satan and a third of the angelic hosts (Isaiah 14.12-15 cf. II Peter 2.4; Jude 6). When Adam and Eve sinned in the Garden of Eden (Genesis 3.1-7), it further corrupted the world; making way for neurotic behavior such as guilt, shame, panic, depression, and anxiety. There are two processes to sin: temptation and transgression (Got hard, Minirth, n.d.). Temptation refers to the internal and external forces that influence how we think, feel, and act. Temptation involve four steps: observation (seeing a thing), desire (thinking about a thing), possession (pursuing a thing), and obsession (lusting over a thing). A transgression is the act of carrying out a temptation. Transgression also involves four steps: thoughts of the mind, temptations of the spirit, desires of the heart, and actions of the body.

In the battle for the control of man, we use defense mechanisms as a way to drive the soul in making a choice on how we should behave.

In the world of psychology, the control of man is caused by the internal urge to act or behave a certain way. In philosophy, behavior is an act of what we believe in or the outcome of our reasoning. In theology, there are external forces that cause man to think a certain way, which cause him to act based on planned thoughts.

As stated earlier, the soul is influenced by internal forces such as the body and the spirit. Like a natural body, the soul uses defense mechanisms (Freud, 1923) in an effort to keep the other two parts of man under control. Some strategies of attack are good and some are bad. These defenses of attack came mostly from Freud's ego-defense mechanisms such as repression (pushing an act or thought into the unconscious), denial (the distorting of actions and thoughts from the conscious), reaction formation (trying to reject a though or action), projection (being possessed by a thought or act), displacement (forward a thought or action to someone else), rationalization (justify a thought or action), sublimation (channel thoughts and actions to something acceptable), regression (having immature thoughts), introjections (taking on the thoughts or actions of someone else), identification (relating to someone else's thoughts or actions), and compensation (masking a thought or act). The final outcome of a behavior rests solely on the soul.

If the soul is influence by the Holy Spirit, the human spirit will become the victor and the body must be subjective to other two parts of man. How do we keep the flesh under subjection so that the soul can be influenced by the spirit to do what is right in the eyes of God and man? First you must want a renewed mind (Romans 12.2). Second, we must place the devil under our feet (James 4.7). Third, we must repent of our sins (II Chronicles 7.14). And last, we must always walk in the spirit (Galatians 5.16-28).

Major of Focus

In Nouthetic-Biblical Counseling must provide an origin for negative behavior in order to develop a system is needed to develop a healthy relationship between counselor and the person or group being counseled. There are three types of approaches a counselor or therapist can used to find the underlying cause of mental illnesses. This systematic attempt to discover the root of a client's crisis is known as The Oscarian Approaches to Problem Detection. There are three elements to this concept:

Holistic approach

Man must be treated of illnesses or disorders holistically: mind or soul, body, and spirit. All three parts of man must be dealt with individually in order to completely cure a person from mental distress (Minirth, 2003). If not, the counselor or therapist only combated the symptoms and not the underlying problem that cause mental and physical ailment in the first place. In fact, most counselors and therapist make their money only by treating the symptoms so they can keep returning to the mental health office with new additions to the same problem. The purpose of The Nouthetic-Biblical Counseling theory is to find ways to solve the problem, not just treating the symptoms.

What good would it be if the therapist deals with only the mind and leaving the body and spirit out of the picture? If a counselor or a therapist only deals with the symptoms and not the problem, the problem will still remain until the root of the crisis is brought up and nullified. That is why prescription drugs don't necessary annihilates the problem because it only deals with the symptoms. There must be other techniques to overcome the problem besides chemicals. It takes both the counselor and counselee to find out the problem in order for a treatment plan can be implemented. The counselor must ask the right questions and tried to open the client's mind. The client must be honest and be willing to explore all avenues of the problem.

Man's distortion of reality causes mental disorders and illnesses which lead to physical health concerns such as hypertension, infections, stroke, diabetes, pain, or even death. Physical ailment can also lead to spiritual brokenness and despair. The alteration of reality is due to the inner struggle to achieve self-actualization. This conflict or an alteration of reality that causes mental and physical infirmities and spiritual decay is call a psycho-dilemma or a psycho powder keg (Williams, 2006). A psycho-dilemma is the breakdown of the holistic man, first with a distortion of reality and decline of mental health, second with physical health problems, and last with a with downtrodden spirit. The breakdown of the spirit is the vulnerable state of man where another force and take over the mental processes for an alternated reality. When that happens, the psycho powder keg explodes, leading to another force or influence to take over the mental state of man from normal to abnormal.

Biblical approach

The Oscarian Theory Series

What does God have to say about human behavior? There are many scriptures in the Bible that deals with everyday behavior such as anger, anxiety, depression, resentment, and self-control.

God's word is the absolute authority in all matters of the mind, body, and spirit. It's a good idea to incorporate the Bible into the therapeutic process in order to find a solution to the big problem: What causes the problem or behavior in the first place? You can do this without burying your religious beliefs on to your patient.

A behavior is more than just an action or reaction, it's comes directly from what we think and feel; whether it's negative or positive. Digging up the dirt on such thoughts could lead to finding the problem. From that point on, a therapist could easily find the problem and match it with the symptoms or behaviors that are associated with the crisis.

Problem-solving approach

Far too often, counselors and psychotherapists often try to deal with the neurological symptoms of an illness or disorder instead of underlying the entire problem.

Prescription drugs only deals with the symptoms but it doesn't get rid of the problem.

Finding a cure for the problem will ultimately cure the mental illness or disorder. There are ways to overcome such setbacks without drugs or humanistic approaches to ridding pain and achieving pleasure (i.e. yoga, spiritism, metaphysics, humanistic philosophy, mythology, and epistemology). Counselors must find the best technique that works for the client that is within ethical guidelines.

Admitting the problem or behavior is the first step to healing. This means that a client has the courage to disclose a psycho-dilemma, alteration of reality that causes a mental or physical sickness, to the therapist along with the symptoms associate with such a crisis. With this information, the therapist can find the best technique to find a solution to the problem not just disposing the symptoms.

The Therapeutic Process: Essential characteristics of a helping relationship

The question concerning counseling and its steps of having a helping relationship with the therapist and counseling is two-fold: First, what is counseling? In summary, counseling refers to a systemized approach in dealing with man, what the way he believes, and what will it take to help an individual achieve self-worth. The nature of man, the presuppositions, and the main focus of the Nouthetic-Biblical Counseling theory, we can finally deal with the second part of the question: what are the most essential characteristics of a helping relationship? According the Nouthetic-Biblical Counseling theory, there is a therapeutic process. This process involves many steps to explain in detail the key elements that must cover in the first session with a new client and why it must be covered.

The therapeutic goals?

Finding the underlying problem and the symptoms and behaviors associated with it whether the problem's origin is from the mind, body, spirit or the entire makeup of man. While prescription drugs

20

may help stop the symptoms, there must be other ways to deal with the crisis holistically. A person's thoughts, reasons, and actions (mind), health of or stress on the flesh (body), and the sense of well-being and worth (spirit) play an important role in overall mental health. There are many kinds of herbs and natural remedies that can be taken with your mental health medication to speed up the recovery process. In fact, these natural supplements can help rid dependency of prescription medicines.

Use theology (particular the Bible) as the foundation or source for the start of the healing process and combine it with traditional forms of counseling and therapy.

Use other techniques of counseling and therapy that works best with the client. Not all techniques of psychotherapy and counseling works for everyone. A counselor or therapist (through a series of tests of assessments) must discover what kind of therapeutic technique works for a client. Find the best possible treatment for the client because not one client is alike.

The functions and roles of the therapist

When it comes to the characteristic of the counselor or therapist, the psychological community is divided on this issue. Theories overtime had a unique set of roles and functions for the therapist. The question is these functions and roles benefiting the counselee or the counselor? When looking for a counselor or therapist, keep these questions in mind.

The characteristics of a good counselor

Consider the Oscarian Characteristics of a Counselor (Adams, et al, n.d.)

A counselor should have a strong belief in God
A counselor should have knowledge of God's word
A counselor should have a godly personality
A counselor should have the fruits of the spirit
A counselor should be able to integrate theology and psychology together
A counselor should know his/her limitation
A counselor should have a mind of confidentiality
A counselor should be transparent
A counselor should weigh all matters spiritually
A counselor should be empathetic not sympathetic
A counselor should know the latest trends in mental health treatment—natural and chemical

What are the characteristics of an effective counselor?

Consider Oscarian Characteristics of an Effective Counselor (Belkin, et al, n.d.)

A counselor should be transparent
A counselor should be trustworthy
A counselor should be open-minded
A counselor should be considerate

The Oscarian Theory Series

A counselor should be three dimensional (empathy, sympathy, fairness)
A counselor should be communicative listener
A counselor should be Knowledgeable and wise
A counselor should be godly
A counselor should be held to the highest standards of ethics and confidentiality.

The function of the counselor?

Consider the Oscarian Functions of a Counselor:

A therapist or counselor must be efficient in the areas of counseling, psychotherapy, and psychology. This person must possess enough knowledge in all three areas to match the symptoms with the problem for a better opportunity to solve the crisis using The Oscarian Approaches to Problem Detection model (the holistic, the biblical, and the problem-solving approach).

It would be helpful if the therapist be experienced in problem-solving not just someone who scratch the surface without finding the root of the problem.

If the therapist has a theological background, it will be a plus in finding a holistic solution to a deeper, inner problem rather than finding the surface of the client's psycho-dilemma. A theological background can be used as the foundation of finding a solution too many mental illnesses most common today such as hyperactivity, depression, schizophrenia, and anxiety.

The function of the therapist is to use the holistic, the biblical, and the problem-solving approaches to finding the problem and the symptoms associated with it (Minirth, 2003). Research is the key to finding problem. A therapist can use one or more techniques, combining it with research and theology, to find a permanent cure for mental illness, disorder, or distress.

The therapist must show empathy for the client and make it a priority to solve the client's crisis so the person doesn't have to return to a mental health facility for the same psycho-dilemma.

What is mentioned by the client must remain with the therapist (Rogers, 1977, Watson, 2002). There must be a strong confidentiality policy between the therapist and the client. If information is to be release to a third party, the client must authorize it in writing.

The client's role in the therapy process? What is expected of the client? What does the client do?

Even though it won't happen in just one therapeutic session, a client must find the courage to share their thoughts, reasoning, and feelings to the counselor.

The counselor and therapist cannot refuse a client for treatment (because of financial or emotional reasons) especially if the person endangers him/herself or other people.

The client must (1) admit to having a problem, (2) want to be help, and (3) work with the therapist to develop goals and a treatment that both parties can agree to.

The nature of the relationship between the client and the therapist

There must be trust between the therapist and the client. The client must be able to trust the therapist with strict confidentiality and be certain that the mental health professional will make the client better.

The client and therapist must be open about any feelings, thoughts, and concerns about the nature of the mental illness, the symptoms associated with such aliment, and treatment options that are available.

The relationship of the therapist and client must be professional at all times. All actions (such as sexual harassment, offensive language, and negative profiling) outside the normal relationship between the client and the therapist are inappropriate.

The therapist must not discriminate on the basis of gender, race, ethnicity, religious background, socioeconomic status, disability, or sexual orientation. All manners of treatment must

be handling on a case-by-case basis non-bialy with the best possible technique to treat a psycho-dilemma. Remember, the counselor or therapist will be dealing with people from all walks of life, so be sensitive about personal looks, the way the individual talks, or what his/her beliefs are.

The members of the counseling team

Consider the Oscarian Counseling Team (Adams and Bogleans, n.d.)

Christ (operation of)
Counselee (the one being counseled)
Circumstance (the problem and its behaviors and conditions)
Counselor (the one who counsels)
Conversation (between counselor and counselee)
Cause (the origin of the problem)
Conversion (by the Holy Spirit)
Change (integration of prayer, problem solving, therapy, and medication)

Techniques and procedures

After identifying the therapeutic process, the Nouthetic-Biblical Counseling theory suggests that an initial session is in order for all new clients. The reason an initial session is need in order to determine the expectations of the client and the therapist so that both parties know what is expected in plain, simple message.

The First Session

Now we can explain in detail the key elements that you must cover in the first session with a new client and why you must cover them.

The Oscarian Theory Series

The first session should always be free and informative. Anything other than that should be regarded to as a red flag.

Introduce yourself, the staff, and your credentials. Let the potential client know you are experience in your feel. Clients need a counselor they can trust.

Mention the role and functions of the therapist. The client needs to know who the counselor or therapy will conduct the session in order for the client to get a feel of the counselor's expertise and techniques.

Mention the role and functions of the client. The client surely will like to how what is expected as simply as possible. By working together with the counselor or therapist, the client will soon be discovered that there is a team that is ready to handle the worse mental cases. This may not be true to the major, but people (in general) longs for rules, procedures, and structure.

Mention how many sessions are needed and how long each session will last. Most sessions should be between one and two hours. Even though these times are acceptable, make sure each session is productive not boring.

Mention the costs that are involve. Make sure they are spelled out completely with no hidden fees. Remember, do an estimate and make sure all fees are written plainly on paper. Clients feel comfortable working with you if counseling/therapeutic firms have this information available. It shows that the clinic cares about not only a client's mental health but the wallet as well.

Mention the principle of confidentiality to a potential client. Make sure you gain the client's trust by keeping the details of all session with the strictest privacy. Make sure you have such a statement in writing.

Allow the potential client to ask questions. Let the person know you want to help in any possible without placing pressure for him/her to commit. It's nothing like old-fashion retail pressure to drive someone way. If a counselor cannot answer the question immediate, the mental health processional should be able to research it and come back later or ask a colleague for help. If any counselor or therapist doesn't do that, its signals a red flag to the client that either the counselor is hiding something or the firm itself is faulty.

The ICT-DSS Method

After the first session, there are six steps used to treat a wide range of mental disorders. That process of the Nouthetic-Biblical
Counseling theory is known as the ICT-DSS Method: identification, control, testing, diagnostic, the self (sharing, empathy, listening, and feeling), and solution. These steps were difficult to developed, but we feel that in order to help anyone (regardless of race), these steps needed to be universal in nature.

The Oscarian Theory Series

1. The Identification Technique

Before doing anything, a therapist must determine if a client has a new mental health case or an existing mental health case. If the client has an existing case, have the client sign a release form authorizing the therapist to obtain information from a third party. Once that information has arrived, the therapist will have some idea about the client's case and can offer the appropriate test for the client to take. If the client has a new case, have the client fill out a questionnaire which should include information such as contact information, nature of mental illness, the symptoms associate with the disorder, and the origin of the ailment. A therapist should receive this questionnaire before any testing can be done.

2. The Control Technique

A client maybe undergoing the symptoms of a mental illness to the point the individual is endangering him/herself or others. If an outburst of abnormal behavior occurs, stop the identification technique and place the client in a controlled environment until the person is calm enough to continue. Return to the identification technique and move forward with the rest of the therapeutic procedures for mental assessment and treatment.

3. The Testing Technique

A therapist can either use the popular psychological testing available. (i.e. Thematic Approach Test, Type A Personality Test, Depression Test, AMPM Personality Test, The Personality Screening Test, The Big 5 Personality Test). There are several tests based on the client's identification of a possible psycho-dilemma. Among the tests are substance abuse, depression, anxiety, bipolar disorder, disassociation disorder, addiction, hyperactivity, stress, personality, relationship, career, and sexual health.

4. The Diagnostic Technique

Depending on what test the client taken, the therapist should look at the questionnaire, any previous records of a client's mental health, and the psychological test to come up with a sound diagnosis. In order develop a reasonable diagnosis, a counselor or therapist must have some knowledge about all areas of mental illness, the symptoms associate with neurological disorders, and some existing techniques used to treat illnesses such as aggression, substance abuse disorder, addictive behaviors, bipolar disorders, hyperactivity, depression, schizophrenia, eating disorders, personality disorders, and anxiety.

5. The Sharing, Empathy, Listening, Feeling (SELF) Technique

Based on what the client's diagnostic is, the therapist can use the SELF Technique (Ellis, 1994, 1997) to ask a series of questions or create hypothetical situations in relationship to the test taken by the client. Technique involves four steps: the client to shares his/her thoughts, concerns, and feelings about reality, the therapist empathically characterizes the client's answers to discover the underlined problem and the symptoms associated with it, the therapist listens to the client's problems and concerns, and the client lashes out his/her feelings in a controlled environment as a way to release stress and tension. These feelings vary from client to client and it's based on the person's diagnostic mental condition.

6. The Solution Technique

There are three things you can do to developing a solution to a client's psycho-dilemma. First, if you are authorized to, prescribe medication to help with the symptoms of the illness. You can also recommend natural herbs and supplements to take with their medication until the client can rid him/herself from prescriptions. You can either see a naturalist or visit a natural health store. Second, get a commitment from the client to develop goals and a treatment plan that both parties can agree to. Third, the therapist should do some homework on the diagnostic illness so he/she would have some idea about what the mental distress the client is suffering from. Four, compile the data collected using the Oscarian Approaches to Problem Detection in order to move closer to the client's treatment. In the holistic approach, the therapist can ask the client what they want to be done to make them better holistically. In the biblical approach, the therapist can use the Bible and find scriptures that deal with everyday commons mental problems such as aggression, addiction, depression, stress, substance abuse, and homosexuality. In the problem-solving approach, the therapist can use the answers from a series of questions; combine it with holistic approach to find the root of the problem. After finding the problem, the client and therapist can work out a plan to holistically treat the client. There should be exercises that help the client move closer to treatment and attainable goals for the client to reach. If the client reaches an achieving goal, a reward of praise and self-worth can be given by the therapist.

Application

After studying the various theories of counseling, which one(s) will you seek to learn more about and use in your own practice of after study the various theories of counseling, Nouthetic counseling and Cognitive biblical counseling will best suit the Nouthetic-Biblical Counseling theory because this school of counseling is based on both theories which has a theological origin combining with cognitive approach in psychology with the integration of the universal system of logic in philosophy.

Choose least two techniques from this theory and explain how and for what client issues you would use them for your clients in treatment.

The Nouthetic counseling theory and the cognitive biblical counseling theory has several techniques that are similar to the integration of both theories. After conducting research on both theories, it's concluded that the Nouthetic and Cognitive biblical counseling theories have much in common and have similar steps in moving the client from irrational thinking and behavior to rational thinking and behavior whose origin is stemmed from theology and psychology.

Nouthetic-Biblical Counseling (NBC) has a wide range of applications that integrate psychology, theology, and philosophy to address both symptom relief and core issue resolution. Some practical applications include:

1. Mental Health Treatment

NBC can be used to counsel individuals struggling with conditions like depression, anxiety, schizophrenia, and phobias by addressing the spiritual, emotional, and cognitive roots of their distress rather than just managing symptoms.

2. Addiction Recovery

NBC principles can be applied in faith-based addiction recovery programs, helping individuals overcome destructive behaviors by integrating biblical truths with psychological techniques that foster behavioral transformation.

3. Pastoral Counseling

Many churches and ministries could implement NBC to assist congregants with spiritual and emotional struggles, offering guidance rooted in Scripture while utilizing psychological insights to promote healing.

4. Marriage and Family Counseling

NBC can be used to strengthen relationships by addressing communication barriers, emotional wounds, and behavioral patterns, integrating faith-based principles with practical counseling strategies.

5. Trauma and Crisis Intervention

NBC can be applied in crisis counseling settings, such as after personal loss, abuse, or major life transitions, to provide individuals with a structured framework for healing that aligns with both psychological recovery and biblical encouragement.

6. Peer Mentorship and Support Groups

NBC can structure peer-based recovery and mentorship programs where individuals help each other navigate spiritual and mental health challenges through guided discussions and accountability.

7. Ethical and Moral Decision-Making in Counseling

NBC offers a foundation for Christian counselors and therapists seeking a balance between professional ethics and faith-based perspectives, ensuring treatment aligns with both theological principles and psychological research.

Peer support and peer recovery support are vital components of the counseling process, especially within the framework of **Nouthetic-Biblical Counseling (NBC)**. These approaches rely on individuals with shared experiences—especially those who have overcome challenges like mental health struggles, addiction, or trauma—to offer encouragement, guidance, and accountability to others on similar paths.

The Oscarian Theory Series

1. The Role of Peer Support in NBC

NBC emphasizes addressing both spiritual and psychological challenges by integrating biblical principles with sound psychological theory. Peer support within this model provides:

- **Encouragement through shared experiences** – Individuals who have faced emotional or spiritual struggles can help others by offering relatable insights grounded in faith.

- **Accountability within a Christian framework** – Scripture-based peer support helps individuals remain committed to healing by reinforcing faith-centered behavioral change.

- **Spiritual mentoring and fellowship** – Peers strengthen each other's journey by applying biblical wisdom to personal transformation.

2. Peer Recovery Support in NBC

Peer recovery support focuses on **helping individuals sustain healing and prevent relapse**, particularly in cases of addiction or emotional distress. NBC applies this concept in:

- **Faith-based recovery programs** – Using NBC principles, peers guide each other toward biblical solutions for enduring psychological and behavioral transformation.

- **Community restoration** – NBC fosters relationships that help individuals reintegrate into spiritual communities, ensuring sustained support beyond counseling sessions.

- **Holistic healing** – Rather than addressing just symptoms, NBC peer recovery support helps individuals uncover deeper spiritual roots of their struggles to achieve complete restoration.

By integrating **peer support and recovery principles with NBC**, individuals find both practical and faith-driven solutions to challenges while receiving compassionate guidance from those who understand their journey firsthand.

Cognitive Counseling – This approach focuses on identifying and modifying dysfunctional thought patterns to improve emotional and behavioral outcomes. It is rooted in cognitive psychology and aims to help individuals reshape negative thinking to develop healthier perspectives and coping mechanisms.

1. **Cognitive-Biblical Counseling** – A faith-based extension of cognitive counseling, this method integrates **biblical principles** with psychological insights. It encourages individuals to align their thoughts with **Christian teachings**, emphasizing renewal of the mind through **Scripture and practical cognitive restructuring techniques**.

2. **Nouthetic Counseling** – Developed by **Jay E. Adams**, nouthetic counseling is a purely **biblical approach** to counseling. It relies on **Scripture alone** for addressing behavioral and emotional struggles, urging repentance and spiritual renewal as the primary means of transformation. It does not incorporate secular psychological theories.

3. **Nouthetic-Biblical Counseling** – Created by **Keith O. Williams**, this theory **integrates psychology, theology, and philosophy** into one comprehensive framework. Unlike traditional nouthetic counseling, **NBC merges theological counseling principles with psychological insights**, allowing therapists to **address both spiritual and cognitive aspects of human behavior** while providing structured methods for diagnosing and treating mental health conditions.

How They Connect

- **Cognitive counseling and cognitive-biblical counseling** both emphasize changing destructive thought patterns, with the biblical model adding a spiritual dimension.

- **Nouthetic counseling and cognitive-biblical counseling** both emphasize Scripture, but **nouthetic counseling rejects secular psychology**, while cognitive-biblical counseling selectively integrates cognitive principles.

- **Nouthetic-Biblical Counseling** unites **cognitive psychology with faith-based teachings**, providing **a holistic approach** that **addresses both spiritual and psychological well-being** rather than focusing solely on either secular or biblical perspectives.

This structured integration makes NBC **a unique, comprehensive model** that offers **flexibility** for counselors while maintaining **theological integrity and psychological effectiveness**.

Notice the chart below how all three theories are related.

Cognitive-Biblical Counseling	Nouthetic Counseling	Nouthetic-Biblical Counseling
Identify problem feeling	Pre-counseling	Identification technique
Identify goal-oriented problem behavior	Pre-counseling	Control technique Diagnostic technique
Identify problem thinking	Pre-counseling	Testing technique
Clarify biblical thinking	Confrontation	Solutions technique
Secure a commitment	Confrontation	Solutions technique
Carry out correct/biblical behavior	Post-counseling	Solutions technique
Identify corrective/Spirit controlled feelings	Post-counseling	Sharing, Empathy, Listening, Feeling (SELF) technique

<u>When and where is the approach most applicable? What types of client would benefit? What types of problem are covered? In what settings does the client feels comfortable in?</u>

The techniques in Nouthetic-Biblical Counseling can be used for almost every type of client. From the mild to the very server cases, a therapist can benefit from using these procedures to cure the client holistically. There are two kinds of distress: those that are caused by a chemical imbalance (mental illness, e.g. depression, anxiety disorders, personality disorders, stress, schizophrenia, etc.) and those that come from the choices we make (habits, e.g. homosexuality, drug and alcohol abuse, gambling, excessive sexual behavior). If a counselor or therapist works in a mental hospital setting, a mental health clinic, or private mental practice, you can use the techniques for both kinds of suffering. The objective is to not only rid the client of the symptoms but also the problem so the counselee will not see the counselor anymore. A therapist cannot assume that the client will be cured in a few sessions. Treating the client will take time, effort, and patience. Nouthetic-Biblical Counseling is used for therapist who wants to offer a long-term plan to treat a client's agony.

<u>What life experience(s) of yours will help you work effectively with a wide range of clients? What are some limitations in your own life experiences that hinder your ability to understand relate to certain clients?</u>

Experience in various mental pathologies such as personality disorders, depression, and bipolar are the main experiences that can be used to relate to most metal health patients. In fact, the vast majority of all mental health abnormalities come from personality (personality disorders), withdrawal (depression), and minor split personalities (bipolar). These common psychological problems give Nouthetic-Biblical Counseling an upper hand in identity, diagnose, and treat these problems effectively. This theory also has another source of information to each psychological pathology is the bible and divine influence by God and His Holy Spirit. No other theories (except for Nouthetic and Cognitive Biblical counseling) have the ultimate source of truth. Anyone who wants to engage in these counseling schools will be able to treat patients holistically: body, mind (soul), and spirit.

However, we must be careful not to fully disclose our past experiences as if a relapse could return at any time. Only a summary of past experiences is acceptable to disclose. Remember, it's not about the therapist. It's about the client. It's might not be a great idea to incorporate your treatment options to the client because it may not work for that individual as the one who receive such treatment. If there is an absolute conclusion that your treatment for past experiences works best with the client, please use them. It might help you and the client.

There have been rumors going around stating that people who have went through a mental disorder or are going through a mental disorder automatically disqualifies someone to counsel others. That is not entirely accurate. In fact, those who have a handle on their mental condition or have been cured of their mental condition are the best candidates to engage in counseling. Who would you prefer to be your counselor: someone who has the personal experience and the education behind it or someone who just have the education but no personal experiences?

In order for a counseling theory to work, the benefits must outweigh the risk.

Evaluation

What is your evaluation of the approach? What are the limitations? What are the unique contributions? Aspects you like most and like and the least?

A major contribution to this theory is the use all schools of thought to treat clients; psychology (to outline the illness and develop a treatment plan), theology (to cater and change the inner portions of man), and philosophy (to think and reason in an attempt to make right choices). If you are looking for a long-term process in treating clients of mental illnesses and destructive habits, this is the theory for you. Secular theorists such as Sigmund Freud and Albert Ellis had some interesting concepts that were integrated into this theory. The SELF Technique, one of six procedures used in the treatment process, was derived from Ellis' thinking, feeling, and acting view of human nature in the cognitive behavioral theory. Freud's three parts of man corresponds with the theological three-fold makeup of man. Christian theorists such as James Dobson and Frank Minirth also integrated theology with philosophy and psychology to develop their theories.

There are a few limitations to this theory. If you are not into a long-term process of treating clients, then this theory is not for you. Some people might criticize this theory because it's design to treat the client of the symptoms and the problem so the individual never have to see a therapist again. Could this mean this treatment option will put all therapists, counselors, psychologists, psychiatrists, and mental health professionals out of work? Many people who work in the psychology field prefer to treat the symptoms and not the problem so their clients keep coming back. That way, the practice will make money. Another limitation is not everyone is a Christian, so this theory might offend some people. Non-Christian clients may not accept this theory because they don't believe in the one that can take all mental stress away, Jesus Christ. So, this theory might not work for everyone is the client is not committed to following this type of treatment option. A final limitation of this theory is the use of ideas from secular theorists. Some Christian counselors may downplay this approach saying it's too much of the world in this theory and not enough Christ.

It's concluded to believe that the entire theory makes sense because many theorists such as Malony, Collins, Crabb, DeVries, Farnsworth, Kirwan, Carter, and Narramore led the way in integrating theology with psychology and philosophy. It's possible to merge all schools of thought into developing a solution to a person's mental anguish. Medication alone will not completely care of person of mental distress. Who can say they are so tired of therapist and counselors treating the symptoms of clients, but these same individuals return to the doctor's office for more sessions that doesn't take care of the root of the problem? After all, money is not important. We can no longer see anyone coming into my office with the same problem over and over again. With millions of people having some form of psychopathic dilemma, it's right to believe that the mental health profession will be in business for a very long time.

What are some specific aspects of this approach (concepts and techniques) that you would most want to incorporate into your own counseling style? Why?

As a person suffering from depression, I truly long for someone to come up with an integrated idea of treating the symptoms and get to the underlying problem: extreme stress. The environment, people, and circumstances give us stress. How I deal with it is either positive (athletics) or negative (neurosis). We should be more interested in the SELF technique as part of the Nouthetic-Biblical Counseling theory because we will have more than enough information to come up with a proper diagnosis and draft up a treatment plan that will completely cure the client once and for all.

In what ways can you apply this approach to yourself personally as a basis for self-understanding and for ideas that you might use in your in your daily life?

After research on the Nouthetic-Biblical Counseling theory, it's safe to say that The Oscarian Approaches to Problem Detection would be the best option to search for a cure for depression, the symptoms and the problem itself. In the holistic approach, we can ask ourselves a series of questions to find out the origin of my illness. In other words, how did someone enter into a state of depression in the first place? In the biblical approach, we would turn to the word of God scripture that deals with depression and seek God's help in healing me from this mental disease. In the problem-solving approach, the answers we receive from God can be integrated with philosophy and psychology to find a cure to depression and all other mental illnesses and destructive habits. In philosophy, we can learn to make better choices by eliminating the outside forces that influence me to behave badly in the first place. The Holy Spirit will have room in your life to influence us to think and act according to God's standards. In theology, we must remember that Jesus Christ bored not only physical illness but mental illness also. Filling my inner self with God will keep my flesh in line with the soul and spirit. In psychology, we could continue to take my medication as prescribed while working with a therapist a plan to rid ourselves of depression. Once the problem is eliminated, we can be taking off the medicines. Holistically, we will be cured.

What client populations do you feel that you would be able to work with and why?

The Nouthetic-Biblical Counseling theory may work on people who have a Christian background or those who independent. With this theory, counselors and therapists are able to find common ground with a non-Christian (by finding some natural thing in common) or with a Christian (their belief and faith in God or their walk with Him). Since Christians are different types of ethnic groups, the Nouthetic-Biblical Counseling theory is the perfect guide to universality among all those who have been saved by Jesus Christ. For the non-Christian however, we can relate to clients on a natural sense (such as our past experiences, interests, and common belief) before we can present the Christian approach. It's good to wait until after a few sessions to move from natural therapeutic processes to supernatural ones.

Placing our Christian beliefs to non-Christians too soon will drive them away and the relationship between client and therapist is lost.

What client populations do you feel you would NOT be able to work with and why?

The Nouthetic-Biblical Counseling theory may not work on people who have religious beliefs that are not Christian in nature. This theory does that deal with people with religions outside religion because such religions such as Hinduism, Islam, and even from Christian denominations such as Mormons and Jehovah Witness' have doctrines slightly or totally opposite of Christianity. Why? There will always be conflicts, violent debates, and rebellion by the counselor and the counselee. It's wise not to take clients who have differences in religious and philosophical views as it will create tension and perhaps violence.

Nouthetic-Biblical Counseling (NBC) is adaptable to various demographic groups, offering tailored approaches based on their specific spiritual, emotional, and psychological needs. Here's how it can be applied to different populations:

1. Youth & Adolescents

- Helps young people navigate identity, peer pressure, and emotional struggles by grounding their perspective in biblical principles and cognitive restructuring.
- Provides a **faith-based framework** for managing anxiety, depression, and social challenges through mentorship and counseling techniques.

2. Adults & Professionals

- Supports individuals dealing with work-related stress, career transitions, and personal crises by integrating psychological coping strategies with scriptural wisdom.
- Strengthens relationships and personal growth through **cognitive-biblical counseling**, addressing thought patterns affecting professional and personal lives.

3. Marriage & Families

- Assists couples in **improving communication**, resolving conflicts, and deepening emotional connections through **faith-centered counseling techniques**.
- Guides parents in biblical-based approaches to raising children, incorporating psychological methods for fostering emotional and behavioral development.

4. Veterans & First Responders

- Provides structured **peer recovery support** tailored to trauma and PTSD, utilizing both **biblical principles** and psychological resilience-building techniques.
- Addresses moral and ethical conflicts experienced in service professions by integrating theology and philosophy with counseling strategies.

5. Women's Counseling

- Offers a **faith-centered healing approach** for women facing life transitions, abuse recovery, and emotional well-being challenges.
- Helps strengthen self-worth and **spiritual empowerment** through biblical counseling practices combined with **cognitive restructuring**.

6. Marginalized & At-Risk Populations

- Supports individuals recovering from **addiction, homelessness, or systemic trauma** by integrating psychology with theological guidance for healing and reintegration.

- Provides faith-based **peer mentorship programs** to help individuals regain stability and purpose through structured recovery models.

7. Senior & Elderly Counseling

- Helps older adults manage **grief, loneliness, and life transitions** through **scriptural encouragement** and cognitive-biblical counseling techniques.

- Supports mental and emotional well-being by integrating **faith-driven reflection and psychological strategies for aging-related concerns**.

NBC's **holistic approach**—combining psychology, theology, and philosophy—ensures that people from **various backgrounds** receive **targeted counseling** that resonates with both their mental and spiritual needs.

While Nouthetic-Biblical Counseling (NBC) is a comprehensive approach that integrates psychology, theology, and philosophy, certain groups may not find it beneficial or compatible with their needs. Here are some cases where NBC may not be the best fit:

1. Individuals Opposed to Faith-Based Counseling

NBC incorporates **biblical principles** alongside psychological techniques. Those who prefer **strictly secular therapy** or reject faith-based perspectives may feel disconnected from its spiritual elements.

2. Those Requiring Intensive Medical or Psychiatric Intervention

NBC is effective for **spiritual and psychological healing**, but individuals with **severe psychiatric disorders**—such as schizophrenia with psychotic episodes, bipolar disorder requiring intensive medication, or neurological conditions—may need **medical and psychiatric care** beyond what NBC offers.

3. People Seeking Non-Integrative Counseling Models

Some counseling models—like **strict cognitive-behavioral therapy (CBT), psychoanalysis, or humanistic therapy**—focus exclusively on psychology without theological integration. Those committed to these methodologies may not see value in the **faith-based aspect** of NBC.

4. Clients Unwilling to Engage in Deep Self-Reflection

NBC requires **active participation** in **self-examination, spiritual reflection, and behavioral change**. Those resistant to self-accountability or unwilling to challenge deeply rooted thought patterns may struggle to engage with its principles.

5. Those Who Reject Philosophical Integration in Counseling

NBC incorporates **philosophical reasoning** alongside theological and psychological concepts. Clients who prefer **strict clinical approaches** without philosophical discourse may feel that the method diverges from their expectations.

The Oscarian Spiritual Concept of the id, the ego, and the superego (2025)

The Breakdown

Sigmund Freud's id, ego, and superego represent different aspects of human personality and behavior, and they can be understood through a spiritual lens in terms of biblical or theological concepts:

1. The Id → The Flesh (Carnal Nature)
The id is driven by primal desires, instinctual urges, and pleasure-seeking behaviors. In a spiritual sense, this parallels the flesh, which represents humanity's sinful nature and unchecked desires.

Scripture often warns against living according to the flesh, which leads to self-indulgence, temptation, and separation from God (Romans 8:6-8).

2. The Ego → The Soul (Self-Identity & Rational Thought)
The ego mediates between the id and superego, balancing desires with reality. Spiritually, this aligns with the soul, which represents conscious decision-making, reasoning, and personal identity.

The soul is where choices are made—between yielding to the flesh (id) or following the spirit (superego).

3. The Superego → The Spirit (Conviction & Moral Guidance)
The superego enforces morality, guiding a person toward ethical living and social rules. Spiritually, this parallels the Holy Spirit or the God-consciousness within, which convicts, guides, and aligns one's actions with righteousness.

The Spirit promotes self-discipline, moral clarity, and obedience to divine principles (Galatians 5:16-25).

How They Connect in Spiritual Growth

The flesh (id) represents human weaknesses and temptations.

The soul (ego) is the battleground for choices between fleshly desires and spiritual guidance.

The relationship with the Nouthetic-Biblical Counseling theory

The Id (Flesh) → Addressing Sinful Desires

NBC acknowledges the fallen nature of humanity, which parallels Freud's id—the source of primal desires and impulses.

Through biblical counseling, individuals learn to recognize and overcome sinful tendencies, replacing destructive impulses with Christ-centered discipline.

The Ego (Soul) → The Battleground of Free Will

NBC views the ego as the mind and will, where moral and psychological choices are made.

This is where cognitive-biblical counseling plays a role—helping individuals process emotions, thoughts, and behaviors in light of spiritual truth.

The Superego (Spirit) → Spiritual Conviction & Moral Guidance

In NBC, the Holy Spirit serves the role of the superego, guiding individuals toward conviction, righteousness, and godly wisdom.

NBC helps people align their thoughts and behaviors with Scripture, reinforcing moral responsibility and ethical decision-making.

Practical Application in NBC

NBC incorporates cognitive restructuring and spiritual transformation to help individuals: ✓ Overcome sinful desires (id) through biblical discipline. ✓ Navigate emotional struggles (ego) through self-examination and theological insight. ✓ Strengthen moral convictions (superego) through scriptural principles and Holy Spirit guidance.

Evaluation

By integrating Freud's psychological framework with Christian theology, NBC offers a holistic approach to healing—one that addresses mental, emotional, and spiritual struggles simultaneously.

The evaluation of **Nouthetic-Biblical Counseling (NBC)** revolves around assessing its **effectiveness, strengths, and limitations** within counseling and psychotherapy. Here's how NBC can be evaluated in relation to its **theoretical foundation, practical application, and interdisciplinary integration**:

1. Theoretical Assessment

✅ **Integration of Theology, Psychology, and Philosophy** NBC merges **biblical principles** with **psychological techniques**, offering a holistic approach that **addresses both spiritual and mental health** concerns. This unique integration makes it **highly adaptable** but requires careful **balancing** between **faith-based** and **scientific methods**.

✅ **Core Framework vs. Other Counseling Models** Unlike secular models (e.g., **cognitive-behavioral therapy, psychoanalysis**), NBC **incorporates theological conviction** into counseling practice. While this **strengthens moral and ethical decision-making**, it may be **less accepted** in strictly clinical settings that prioritize empirical evidence over spiritual guidance.

2. Practical Application

✅ **Strengths**:

- **Addresses Root Causes, Not Just Symptoms** – NBC seeks to uncover **spiritual, emotional, and cognitive origins** of distress rather than merely **managing behaviors**.

- **Faith-Based Healing & Accountability** – Encourages **community and peer support**, reinforcing **long-term recovery** through spiritual guidance.

- **Comprehensive Treatment Model** – Can be **tailored** to multiple demographic groups, including **youth, veterans, families, and marginalized communities**.

⚠️ **Potential Challenges**:

- **Resistance from Non-Faith-Based Clients** – Individuals who do not embrace **theological principles** may struggle to connect with the framework.

- **Limited Scientific Validation** – While NBC **incorporates psychology**, it has not been widely studied in controlled clinical trials, making empirical validation more challenging.

- **Counselor Training Requirements** – Counselors using NBC **must be knowledgeable** in **psychology, theology, and philosophy**, making competency essential for successful application.

3. Interdisciplinary Evaluation

- **Psychological Perspective**: NBC aligns with **cognitive-based approaches** but goes beyond symptom relief by integrating theological counseling techniques.

- **Theological Perspective**: It strengthens **spiritual development**, applying biblical truths for inner transformation.

- **Philosophical Perspective**: NBC **engages with existential and ethical questions**, creating a foundation for **self-reflection and purposeful living**.

Final Consideration

NBC offers **a dynamic and faith-centered approach**, addressing **both spiritual and psychological healing**. While it has **broad applications**, its effectiveness depends on **the openness of clients, the counselor's expertise**, and **the integration of interdisciplinary principles**.

Evaluating the **spiritual concept** of Freud's **id, ego, and superego** requires examining how these elements align with theological, philosophical, and psychological perspectives within **Nouthetic-Biblical Counseling (NBC)**. Here's a structured analysis:

1. The Id – The Flesh (Carnal Nature & Human Temptation)

◆ **Biblical Alignment** – The **id** represents raw, instinctual desires, akin to the **"flesh"** in Scripture, which is prone to **sin, impulsivity, and worldly temptations** (Romans 8:6-8). ◆ **NBC Perspective** – NBC acknowledges that **human nature** carries inherent weaknesses, but through **biblical discipline and spiritual renewal**, individuals can **overcome destructive desires** and redirect them toward godly living. ◆ **Evaluation** – While Freud saw the **id** as an uncontrollable force, NBC teaches that **spiritual transformation** can reshape desires through **Scripture, prayer, and conscious effort**.

2. The Ego – The Soul (Free Will & Rational Thought)

◆ **Biblical Alignment** – The **ego** serves as the mediator between impulses and moral principles, resembling the **soul**, which is the seat of **self-awareness, reasoning, and decision-making** (Joshua 24:15). ◆ **NBC Perspective** – NBC integrates **cognitive-biblical counseling** to help individuals **renew their thinking**, allowing the soul (ego) to function **in harmony with both wisdom and faith** rather than merely balancing fleshly desires. ◆ **Evaluation** – Freud emphasized **ego as rational control**, but NBC views it as **the battleground for spiritual choices**, where faith **guides rational thought** rather than relying purely on self-determined morality.

3. The Superego – The Spirit (Conviction & Divine Guidance)

◆ **Biblical Alignment** – The **superego**, which enforces morality, parallels the **Holy Spirit**, which **convicts, instructs, and leads believers toward righteousness** (John 16:13). ◆ **NBC Perspective** – NBC highlights the **superego's role in moral formation**, connecting it to the **Holy Spirit's influence on personal and ethical development**. Instead of merely adopting societal norms, **NBC promotes alignment with divine principles** as the highest moral authority. ◆ **Evaluation** – Freud viewed **superego morality as socially conditioned**, whereas NBC **sees spiritual conviction as God-ordained**—guiding individuals toward **absolute truth rather than cultural constructs**.

Final Assessment in NBC

NBC **reframes Freud's structure** through **theological integration**, recognizing: ✓ The **id** (flesh) as an obstacle to overcome through **spiritual discipline**. ✓ The **ego** (soul) as the battleground for **faith-based rationality and decision-making**. ✓ The **superego** (spirit) as the source of **divine moral guidance, higher than mere social norms**.

NBC **bridges psychology with Christian counseling**, offering **a transformative approach** that **aligns personality theory with biblical truth**—making **spiritual renewal** the ultimate goal of counseling rather than merely behavior modification.

References

Books (Print & E-Books)

Williams, K. O. (2025). *The Oscarian Theory Series*. Greater Works Publishing. Williams, K. O. (2025). *Nouthetic-Biblical Counseling: A New Approach to Therapy*. Greater Works Publishing.

Edited Books

Crabb, L. J. (Ed.). (2010). *Biblical counseling perspectives*. Zondervan.

Journal Articles

Adams, J. E. (2006). Biblical counseling and psychology. *Journal of Christian Counseling, 12*(3), 45-60. https://doi.org/10.xxxx

Kindle Books

Ellis, A. (1999). *Thinking, feeling, and acting: A cognitive approach*. Harper & Row.

Biography

Keith Oscar Williams was born on April 25, 1974, in Birmingham, Alabama. The third of five children, he was raised by his father, **Albert Williams Sr.**, a skilled fabricator, and his mother, **Dorothy Leon Hampton**, a dedicated homemaker.

Williams graduated from **A.H. Parker High School** in 1992 before pursuing higher education at **Alabama State University, Miles College, the University of Alabama-Birmingham, and Liberty University**. His academic journey also includes several religious degrees from **World Bible School, Cathedral University, and Grace and Truth Bible Institute**.

A proud **U.S. Army veteran**, Williams served during the Gulf War campaign at **Fort McClellan, Alabama**, in the late 1990s. Beyond his military service, he is a visionary leader, founding **Greater Works Business Services (1998), Great I Am Ministries Outreach International (2003), and the internet radio station OBS (2007).**

Williams' literary career began in **1991** with his first poem, *The Old Oak Tree*. Over the years, he has penned numerous thought-provoking works, including *My Broken Heart (1992), Keith Loves Tamikia (1993), Julie's Alright (1994), Delilah in an Unknown Place (1995), Starting Over Again (1997), The Irvina Lullaby (1998), The Tulip Song (1998), and Celebrate Love (2003)*.

In **August 2004**, he published his first book, *The True Experience, Volume I*, a collection of over 100 poems filled with **spiritual and inspirational messages of hope, encouragement, and patience**. His other works include *Spirit Led, Spirit Fed (2006), Lessons for Life (2008), The Oscarian Theory Series (2010), and The World of Christian Doctrine, Volumes 1-3 (2013)*.

With several upcoming books—including *The True Experience, Volumes II & III, A Series of Fortunate Spiritual Events, and King Edward's Courtyard*—Williams continues to shape the literary landscape.

Today, he resides in **Birmingham, Alabama**. He was previously married to **Sheona Tibbs** of Fredericksburg, Virginia. The couple wed in **2001**, remained together for **15 years**, and finalized their **divorce in 2016**.

At present, Williams serves as a **minister, writer, activist, and entrepreneur**, continually making an impact through his work and vision.